The Basilica of Aquileia is a place of spiritual and artistic tradition.
Central to the spiritual tradition is Easter, namely, the death and the resurrection of Jesus Christ, the pivotal event of Christian belief. It does not recall the past, but instead a living presence in the church community that continues to be united, every Sunday, by the sacrament of the Eucharist.

The language of fine arts gives rise to this pictorial tradition, through which the mystery of Easter is expressed in a myriad of ways. Such variety speaks for the effort to take diverse cultural and historical facts into account.

The strong message can incite worship as well as wonder, conjure forth existential questions or arouse scientific interest, and promote responsible tourism or a cultural passion.

Depending upon the visitor's particular state of mind and outlook on life, he or she can feel at home here in this sacred place. Those who come here will be received by the Mother of God, who gazes lovingly out from the apse and points towards Jesus, her Son, who said, „I am the way, the truth, and the life."

+ Dino De Antoni

+ Mons. Dino De Antoni
Archbishop and Metropolitan of Gorizia

Aquileia

The Basilica
A Brief Guide

City: Aquileia   Country: Italy

Preface

Dear Visitors,
Welcome to the Basilica of Aquileia.
The Basilica offers you the opportunity for an extraordinary human experience, of a tour through history, one which is led singularly by the beauty of art and the expression of spirituality.
This guide will provide you with an appreciation of the countless witnesses to a rich spiritual and cultural tradition, whose roots extend back over the Roman colonization of Aquileia in 181 B.C.
Allow yourself to be accompanied by the simple words of the guide, but above all, by the stillness of the rooms, in which you can hear the gentle and melancholy voices of time. Those who were in this place before us wished to convey an important message that wants to be heard and above all, experienced. With this in mind, we wish you a wonderful visit and hope that you will return again to the Basilica soon.

An Overview of the Basilica ❶

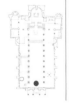

After you enter the basilica, please remain upon the glass brid¬ which was installed in 2000 in order to protect the valuable flo mosaics. We suggest that you remain here for a moment and allo yourself to be taken in by the celebratory breadth of the room. single glimpse can encompass nearly 1700 years of history. The vie

may be hidden, but you can imagine the Roman houses which stood in front of the basilica structure, as well as the signs of a pre-Christian and Jewish religious past that extended across the old city.

The 4th century A.D. is worth a closer look. The original church of Aquileia was built at the time of Bishop Theodore soon after the Edict of Milan in 313, by which Emperor Constantine proclaimed the freedom to decide one's faith and made the construction of Christian churches possible. The church consisted of two parallel halls which were connected by a third hall. Possibly, it was with the south church - in which you are standing now - that was adorned with large floor mosaics, and its borders were the columns to your left, the commencement of the stairs leading to the altar, and the right external wall reserved for the catechumenate. Meanwhile, the celebration of the Eucharist took place in the north church that is now partially incorporated into the campanile. Like many old churches, the Basilica is also oriented towards the east. Its altar room thus faces the east, where the sun rises; for the early Christians, the sun was a symbol for Jesus Christ, the star of justice.

It is possible that under Bishop Chromatius (387/388–407/408), a new church was built, which in terms of its dimensions is comparable to the current church. The level of the brick pedestals, upon which the nave columns stand, corresponds to the second floor that fully covers the first. As you move towards the altar, you can see via two openings a few smaller fragments of the large floor mosaic created during Chromatius' reign.

An additional reconstruction of the Basilica was led by Patriarch Maxentius in the 9th century. He ordered the addition of a crypt for the relics of the countless martyrs from Aquileia, which required the elevation of the presbytery and the insertion of a transept.

Under Patriarch Poppo, a renovation was needed and completed with the re-dedication of the Basilica on July 13, 1031. The church was adapted to what was then a modern style and fitted with Roman round arches as well as a splendid half-dome. From it, the Mother of God with the infant Jesus in her arms, the symbols of the Evangelist the holy martyrs, the patriarch, Emperor Conrad, and the powerful figures of the age look down upon you.

In 1348, Patriarch Marquard had the church restored after it had been severely damaged in Friuli's frequent earthquakes, the most recent traces of which were left upon the walls. Needless to say, he also wished to be "modern" and thus consulted the Gothic architects, as clearly demonstrated by the peaked arches between the columns. The Renaissance style was taken next into account between the end of the 15 and the first half of the 16th century with the right tabernacle, in which

the most holy sacrament of all was kept. The beautiful nave ceiling in the form of a ship's keel originates from this period, as well as the transept ceiling which bears a wooden plaque of 1560. At the beginning of the 20th century, 1909 to be precise, the floor mosaic was discovered and the overlying floor of the basilica was removed. In doing so, the church lost its harmonious medieval proportions, while on the other hand, its most significant hidden treasure was brought to light.

The glass bridges that were installed a few years ago bear witness to a new interaction with the Basilica, which is not so much liturgical as tourist-oriented. It allows you to comprehend the fantastic floor mosaics with one singular look, to traverse it with your eyes if not literally, and enables you to be led through the Garden of Eden via the symbols of its artists.

Now discover the most significant "secrets" of the mosaics created under Theodore.

The Cock and the Turtle ❷

As you proceed a few meters to the right, you will notice a square beneath the junction of the glass bridge, in which can be seen a somewhat faded but still-recognizable cock and turtle who appear to fight over a prize contained within a trapezoid atop a column.

The cock, who crows before the break of day, is the symbol for Jesu
Christ, with whom the new day of life and the resurrection begin. B
contrast, the turtle as the creature of the underworld personifies th
divisive character of heresy who cannot recognize the light of truth
There are a number of symbols within the trapezoid. Among thes
include the sideways eight, which may stand for eternity, as well a
three Cs (CCC) that recall the Roman numeral 300 and whose Gree
equivalent is the tau symbol (similar to a cross). In a sermon about
famous Biblical story, Bishop Chromatius claimed that Gideon cor
quered a large army of Amalekites with the aid of only 300 compa
nions, for the number 300 prefigures the power of Christ's triump
over death.

As a result, a number of archaeologists have given the mosaic of th
cock and turtle a dating after the year 381. In that year, the Basilic
held the so-called Council of Aquileia, in which individuals such a
Saint Ambrose and Saint Valerianus participated. Over its course, th
ideas of the heretical Arian teachings were judged, which were repr

sented at the aforementioned time by bishops Palladius and Secondianus.

A view towards the south outer wall allows you to recognize the unusual contour of a face beneath the countless preserved images in front of the 15ᵗʰ-century baptismal font. The face looks towards the west and spits upon the ground. It recalls the position where the catachumen, before he was allowed to enter the place of baptism, had to scornfully renunciate three times Satan, evil, and sin.

The "Donors" and the Good Shepherd ③

Proceed towards the presbytery, but on your way, remain standing at the splendid representation of the shepherd on your right and the faces on your left.

The shepherd on the right side of the bridge is slightly elevated from the ground and holds a wind instrument, a pan flute, in his hand. He carries a sheep upon his shoulders, while an additional sheep stands

upon the grass. The symbol, which is typical for Christian iconography of that period, is intended to recall the resurrected Christ who has ascended to Heaven and lovingly watches over the heavenly Church that has already set aside its material path. Meanwhile, the military church, with its legs firmly set upon the ground, regards its reason for being as contemplating the face of the shepherd. To the right can be seen an antelope, an animal from the south; at the left is a deer representing an animal from the north. This arrangement emphasizes the centrality of Christ, the "center of the cosmos and of history." Within the scene can be seen fish and birds, as well as a struggle between an ibex, a turtle, and a snake, which perhaps calls to mind orthodoxy and heresy, or more generally, the conflict between good and evil.

A similar message is conveyed by the expressive faces upon the left side of the glass bridge, which at the same time call forth a number of questions. Especially unclear are whose faces they represent and in particular, who the man in the middle is supposed to be. Some assume that it is the beardless Jesus Christ, who is adorned with the imperial insignia and surrounded by His disciples. For others, by contrast, it portrays Emperor Constantine with his court. Still others

believe it is simply a tribute to the donor who made the construction of the church possible. Be that as it may, the surrounding faces appear to be personifications of the four seasons - especially recognizable are fall and summer - which are typically arranged around important images of the Redeemer or the history of salvation. Also very frequent is the illustration of a fish, a symbol for Christ during the persecutions, when Christians regarded the Greek word ἰχθύς as an acronym for Jesus Christ, God's Son, Savior; the fish also symbolized the Christians, who joined the church through baptism "sicut pisciculi" (Tertullian).

A few steps away from this field of mosaics you will find another unusual mosaic which merits a closer look.

The Triumph of Christianity ❹

A winged female figure is shown holding a laurel wreath and palm branch in the middle of the mosaic. At her feet are two baskets, one with grapes and another (severely damaged) with wheat ears. Some researchers believe it to be an image of the goddess of triumph, for in

the Roman world, the emperor who returned victorious from batt
was crowned with a laurel wreath.

By contrast, the palm branch likely recalls Christ's Entry into Jerusa
lem, as well as the palms carried after the Apocalypse by those wh
had shed blood for the Lamb of God.

Around the central figure are grouped ten figures, who present th
fruits of their labor and carry them to the altar.

The depiction may be interpreted as follows: human labor is conve
ted into bread and wine; the death and resurrection of Christ agai
transforms the bread and wine into the body and blood of Jesus whic
is present in the ritual; through the participation in the sacrament
the Eucharist, the people receiving the sacrament in turn incorpora
Christ back into their daily work.

To the left and right areas of the image are numerous animals, but
is difficult to give an individual symbolic meaning to each on
Perhaps they embody the "mystical herd of Christ" or the people wh
followed Jesus and having triumphed, have earned the eternal rewar
of heavenly pastures.

The Jonah Mosaic ❺

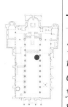

*The Jonah Mosaic, which you will reach next, is the largest mosa
representation upon the floor of the Basilica and covers the entir
eastern section. Before you explore the meaning of the image, immers
your thoughts into the ocean full of fish and allow yourself to becom
mesmerized by its shimmering variety.*

In the ocean are numerous fish, beautiful and ugly, good and ba
One of them is a sea monster which devours everything alive. Thi
includes a man thrown from a boat, from which a praying man ob
serves the entire scenario, his arms extended to the heavens. In th
scene beneath beneath the glass bridge, the evil fish spits out the ma
upon the beach. The same man later rests beneath an arbor wit
pumpkins dangling overhead.

The meaning of this depiction is revealed in the Gospels. There, Jesu
Christ tells the story of his death and resurrection from the Hebre
Bible. "For as Jonah was three days and three nights in the fish'
belly, so shall the Son of God remain three days and three nights i
the bowels of the earth." The story of Jonah – who is sent from Go
to return to Nineveh, who escapes to a ship from which he is cast int
the water to prevent its destruction by the approaching storm, who i

then devoured by the sea creature and spit out, ultimately to return unexpectedly to the city – is the story of all living things, who sooner or later will be consumed by the monster of death. Jesus Christ triumphs over death, in that the evil fish cannot retain him. In his glory, He expects that all will participate in redemption, which can only succeed when they "allow themselves to be pulled from the water." It involves a clear reference to baptism at a time when the bishop "pulled from the water" the catachumens who approached the church with trepidation.

The round area in the middle alludes to the fact that, among other things, Bishop Theodore built all of these edifices "with the help of God and the herd which was entrusted to him by heaven."

Take leave of the glass bridge and continue your tour at the marb[le] slab of the beautiful medieval floor.

The South Chapel ❻

Turn now to the right and view the small chapel, which is embedde[d] into the south outer wall.

The chapel dates to 1493 and is dedicated to Saint Jerome, who fro[m] 370 to 373 A.D stayed in Aquileia and actively participated in the li[fe] of the local Christian community. He also established close ties wit[h] countless important representatives of the Latin Church of his tim[e] particularly with Chromatius, Rufinus, and Heliodorus.

In the middle of the chapel stands a painted stone sculpture, a piet[à] from the middle of the 15th century. Its stylistic characteristics and i[ts] chronological placement suggest an Austrian origin, where this ico[no]nographic type was typical and widespread.

A few meters away, the beautiful Torriani Chapel dedicated to Ambros[e] deserves your attention.

Its walls date back to the 11th century, where it served as a sma[ll] church inside the Basilica, as evidenced by the Gothic-style vaultin[g] and the lamb at its center. In 1298 at the request of Patriarch Rai[-]mondo of the Torre family, it was refurbished as a funeral chapel f[or] him and select members of his family. As a result, the constructio[n] was significantly altered and was named the Ambrose or Torrian[i] Chapel.

Inside, a door leads to an imposing grille, behind which four sarco[-]phagi stand. Tradition holds that Raimondo is buried in the red mar[-]ble sarcophagus (the first on the left), upon which he is shown i[n] bishop's robes, with a dragon at his feet, and along the sides of hi[s] head, two angels who scatter incense. In the other tombs rest th[e] treasurer Rainald (the second on the right), Patriarch Paganus (th[e] second on the left), and Patriarch Ludovicus (the first on the right[). Between the two tombs on the right is a gravestone in memory o[f] Allegranza of Rho (who died in 1300), the mother of Rainald an[d] Patriarch Gaston.

Through the restoration of 2000, it was possible to confirm the hypo[-]thesis that chapel had first been reconstructed in the year of Rainald['s] death (1332). This would have required his tomb to be placed beneat[h] an arch in the south wall and the chapel to be decorated with frescoe[s]. In fact, the arch of the south wall (which is now partially immured[)]

had the exact dimensions needed to accommodate Rainald's sarcophagus and features frescoes displaying Saints Hermagoras and Ambrose, who are also seen in the Crucifixion scene (13th c.) at the east wall. With the restoration of the south wall, the two symmetrically arranged oval windows and the altar beneath it, all from the 18th century, were improved.

At the end of the right transept arm, you will find the chapel dedicated to Saint Peter.

The Chapel of Saint Peter contains original 14th-century frescoes which form the background for the restored polyptych by Pellegrino of San Daniele.

Splendid Lombard chancel tiles from the 9th century form the precious framework for the chapel. They belong to the transenna (barrier) which bordered the presbytery during the Early Middle Ages.

In the half-dome, a "Christ in Majesty" is displayed, surrounded by four saints who are difficult to identify. Far beneath is the "Volto Santo," the original image of a crucified Christ clothed in a Byzantine garment, which may have been modeled after an older image from the Cathedral in Lucca.

The polyptych is the most important piece by Pellegrino da San Daniele (1467-1537), one of the most significant Renaissance artists from the Friuli area. The work, which was completed in 1503, is the result of a collaboration among Pellegrino, Giovan Pietro da Udine, and

Antonio Tironi. It completed the project of modernization of the presbytery according to the Renaissance style which had begun in 1479.
It was Patriarch Domenico Grimani who commissioned the polyptych
in order to decorate the main altar and to both salvage and conceal
the Istrian stone Mother of God, the *Virgo lactans*, behind the higher
central wing. This can now be viewed at the altar of Saint Hilary. The
polyptych consists of three components, each depicting a pair of
saints. On the left are Saints Hermagoras and Fortunatus, in the
middle are Saints Peter and Paul, and on the right are Saints George
and Hieronymus. The entire work incorporates scenes which recall the

rise of the Church of Aquileia. The figure of the risen Christ in the curved panel over the central wing is flanked by Isaiah and David.

After the restoration work of the apse frescoes was completed in 1921, the polyptych was initially installed in the Ambrose or Torriani Chapel. Since the end of its restoration (from 1998 to 2005), it has been located in the Chapel of Saint Peter.

The Maxentius Crypt (Crypt of the Frescoes)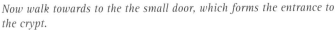

Now walk towards to the the small door, which forms the entrance to the crypt.

The Crypt of the Frescoes, which was built at the request of Patriarch Maxentius in the 9th century, has a semicircular layout. It is divided by two rows of columns which support the three-aisled vaulting. It is meant to contain the sarcophagus with the relics of the martyrs of Aquileia, Hermagoras, and Fortunatus. This was located precisely in the middle of the crypt, protected by iron bars between the columns. The still-visible holes in their shafts indicate their position.

The crypt receives light – as much as its position allows - through three windows which open in the east wall of the chapel. Between the middle and the two side windows, two small rooms, which likely functioned as the sacristy in earlier times, are located in the lower section.

At the height of the altar, by contrast, a fourth window which extends to the interior of the basilica can be seen. This involves the so-called "fenestella confessionis," which served one important purpose for the faithful. Turned toward this tiny window, they "confessed and confided" to their faith and recalled the examples of the two saints, especially on July 12th, the anniversary of their martyrdom.

At the sides of the altar, it is possible to catch a glimpse of the martyrs of Aquileia. Contained within two reliquaries adorned with filigree work and lapis lazuli, they demonstrate that the memory of them is alive within the community.

Although the crypt was built in the 9th century, its frescoes were not created until some centuries later.

Within the crypt, there is a sensation of being literally "encased" by the frescoes; the ceiling and side walls are in fact, completely covered. Although ambiguities prevail as to their origin, many researchers are convinced that they were created with a certain stylistic consistency at around the end of the 12th century by one or more unknown artists.

To understand this, it is necessary to differentiate between the ceiling frescoes and those of the side lunettes.

Aside from the representations of Christ between two saints, the Virgin Enthroned, and Saint Hermagoras between the saints Fortunatus and Syrus within the central aisle, the twenty-three connecting scenes relay the so-called "Cycle of Mark" according to the Christian message first proclaimed by Saint Mark in Aquileia. Having arrived in the city, Mark met Hermagoras and impressed by his faith, accompanied him to Rome so that he could be ordained bishop by Saint Peter. Upon his return to Aquileia, Hermagoras made Fortunatus deacon; together they continued to serve as apostles, which ultimately led to their imprisonment. However, during the years of their confinement, they continued to baptize and convert many people and in this manner strengthened the belief of the community. After they were sentenced to death and decapitated, they were buried by their disciples.

The side lunettes, which are unfortunately quite damaged, depict episodes from the Passion (Crucifixion, Deposition, and Entombment) and encompass the suggestive display of a *Dormitio Virginis*. Worth noting here is the connection between the majestic, yet theologically rigid iconographic scheme of Byzantine art and the sculptural representation of human emotions typical of early Italian art. The lower section is also interesting, revealing frescoes of horsemen, archers and various animals whose interpretation is not straightforward, and who are protected by a curtain-like structure. They recall the frescoes from the sacred buildings in Friuli-Venezia Giulia and other areas which could suggest a dating of the early 13th century.

Take another last look at the frescoes and continue on your tour.

The Apse ⑧

Exit the crypt and climb the steps to the altar and chancel, an ideal spot from which to admire the wonderful frescoes of the main apse. Nevertheless, take a moment to enjoy the breathtaking view of the nave before looking up towards the half-dome.

You are standing in front of a majestic fresco which was commissioned by Patriarch Poppo in 1031. At its center, the Mother of God is enthroned within a mandorla with the infant Jesus upon her arm. She is surrounded by the symbols of the Evangelists (at the top are an angel, an eagle, beneath her are an ox and a lion). At the sides of the Madonna in Majesty are depictions of figures important to Aquileia's

Christian tradition. Within this group are saints Hermagoras and Fortunatus (the first martyrs and city patrons) as well as Saint Euphemia. Between them, rendered in smaller scale, are three individuals who were still alive at the time of the work's completion, namely, Emperor Conrad II, his wife, and his son. Upon the left side of the Mother of God are Saint Mark, whose hand is extended towards her, and saints Hilary and Tatian (who, according to tradition, were bishop and deacon and served as the successors to Hermagoras and Fortunatus). Between them are Poppo, with the square halo, and probably Ozi, the brother of the patriarch.

The lower section is dominated by majestic figures of other martyrs from Aquileia, while an inscription in Gothic lettering within a red scroll indicates the names and origins of the bishops who were present at the dedication of the Basilica on July 13, 1031.

Before you move on to the left transept arm, remain for a moment at the chancel which was designed by Bernardino da Bissone in 1491. From here, the patriarch "embraced" the faithful and spread the Word of God. The majestic character of this church – which becomes clearly evident at this spot – is wholly interwoven with the grandeur and significance of the patriarchs of Aquileia.

The Left Transept Arm

Now descend the steps of the altar room, walk beneath the large organ (donated in 1896 by the Austrian Emperor Franz Joseph) and enter the Chapel of Saint Hilary at the end of the left transept arm.

Behind the altar are frescoes depicting Bishop Hilary and the deacon Tatian along with Largius, who was probably a monk about whom no further information has survived. Although it is not known who completed the frescoes, a certain similarity to the apse frescoes has been identified, leading to the assumption that the date as well as the artists were identical. Also worth noting are the other wall frescoes and the flat relief in front of the altar from the 14th century depicting Christ with Peter on his left and the holy bishop Thomas of Canterbury on his right. Donated to the patriarchs of Aquileia, it bears witness to the international relationships between the old European churches. The chapel organ from 2001 is often played at major concerts which take place during the summer.

The Left Aisle ❿

Upon leaving the chapel, you will discover the recessed figure of "Christ in the Trench," a wholly dramatic modern sculpture which was made by Edmondo Furlan in 1917. It recalls the difficult times endured by the people in this area during the First World War. A few steps further along is the Chapel of the Rosary in the left aisle. At the tabernacle, an eternal light burns, indicating the sacrament of the Eucharist, the heart of every Catholic Church, and encouraging a respectful silence at the place of prayer.

The chapel was built in the 18th century and was only recently restored. Within it is the single Baroque work of the patriarchal basilica, an altar leaf which was made by the canon Giuseppe Cosatti of Aquileia in the 17th century and displays the Madonna of the Rosary between John the Baptist and Dominic.

A few steps further, you will find a splendid artwork which is hard to miss.

The large, delicately-carved wooden cross, which has been inserted into a niche, has been assigned to the 15th century by most researchers. It unleashes not only a deep spirituality and a great inner joy, but is also venerated as a miracle worker by the local community. Because of this, it was once carried at the front of processions through the fields during extended dry spells.

As you take a look around and direct your gaze to the floor, it is still possible to admire a number of mosaics beneath the benches which recall those of the central nave and therefore, date to the era of Theodore. Dominating the image are the fish who appear to swim to the sea of Jonah. The mosaics were removed for restoration and reinstalled in an elevated position.

Now descend the steps which will lead you to the original level of the basilica. Before you enter the so-called "Excavation Crypt," take another look at the unusual cylindrical construction of Greek marble, with which the copy of the Holy Sepulcher in Jerusalem was made. It was initiated by Patriarch Poppo and completed for the 1000th death anniversary of Jesus in 1033. Because Aquileia was located along the Via Romea which leads pilgrims from Central and Eastern Europe to Rome and Jerusalem, Poppo benefited from the descriptions of Christ's grave which were relayed to him, constructing an exact, albeit smaller copy of the Holy Sepulcher of Jerusalem. It is possible that sketches from the diary of a pilgrim named Arculf also helped him in the process. In the monument's interior is a small altar upon a pillar and a slab with three round recesses varying in size. Only the middle one is open. In the Holy Sepulcher of Jerusalem, these allowed the faithful to confirm that the grave was indeed empty. The Holy Sepulcher of Aquileia fulfilled and continues to fulfill a liturgical function that is tied to Holy Week and the celebration of Easter.

Next to the entrance of the grave, a small door leads to the Excavation Crypt, which was installed in 1917 and has been worked on several times since then.

The North Hall  ⓫

The Excavation Crypt gives you the impression of standing in a room dating to the 1ˢᵗ to 4ᵗʰ centuries, which had been buried and just recently discovered.

The glass bridge runs at the level of the middle room, which having once connected the south and north hall of Theodore, was partially destroyed owing to subsequent buildings. Some researchers have characterized this room as a "consignatorium," for in ancient times, the bishop might have bestowed the sacrament of confirmation upon the newly baptized. From the location of the glass bridge, some of the various construction levels can be seen. The first belongs to a house from the 1ˢᵗ century, in which the mosaics with geometric figures are visible, as well as a number of aqueducts that were used at a later time to provide water to the baptismal font of Theodore. The second level, which for the most part has been replaced by the modern glass strips, is the level of the Cocciopesto floor of the middle room. Lastly, the third room, which following its discovery was elevated via cement supports at the beginning of the 20ᵗʰ century, is that of the post-theodorian north hall, which was built at about the middle of the 4ᵗʰ century at the initiative of Bishop Fortunatian and was solemnly dedicated by the patriarch Anathanasius of Alexandria, who was banned during the Arian controversy.

One door with an original sill leads you to the north hall of the 4ᵗʰ century basilica, the place which contains the most artistically signi-

*ficant and at the same time, most cryptic mosaics. As soon as yo
enter the room, you will notice a large wall which sinks into the floc
mosaics. It is a foundation of the campanile that was built in the 11
century at the time of Patriarch Poppo. As demonstrated by a numbe
of stones with ancient inscriptions, material from some of the col
lapsed Roman buildings was used.*

The first mosaics you see are not all that impressive, even though
number of original details, i.e., the basket with mushrooms and th
snails next to the glass slab, are visible upon further inspection. Ther
is also a row of inscriptions which merits attention. One of the less
visible inscriptions which reads, "Ore felix hic crevisti, hic felix" ma
have been in memory of "the happy (Theodo)rus, who grew up her
and was happy." In another inscription located beneath a corner o
the campanile, it notes that "Ianuarius de dei dono v(ovit) r
DCCCLXXX"or, "Januarius, with the gift of God, you donated 880
(which amounts to approximately 26 square meters of land, possibl
for the construction of the church).

In contrast, the mosaics located in the narrow passage between th
north outer wall and the campanile contain several interesting inter
pretations. Without a doubt, these mosaics are an expression of th
unusual theological vitality of Aquileia's church community at tha
time and its consolidated close relationships with the other churche
of early Christianity, especially with that of Alexandria in Egyp
However, the current state of knowledge regarding the absolute origi
nality of the iconographic schemes calls for circumspection, eve
though it may be perfectly legitimate to construct parallels betwee.
the artistic representations and some of the most important works c
ancient spiritual literature.

Among the unusual portrayals are the screeching donkey, which bear
the sign of bishopric dignity, the purple hens opposing it, and severa
trees in the form of a tau cross, upon which billy goats, a partridge nes
and a crayfish are located. In the north corner of the campanile is
powerful ram with a white blaze, over which can be seen the inscriptio
"Cyriace vibas", which may have been directed to a Christian by th
name of Cyriacus or to the baptized, each of whom becomes the Ma
of Kyrie, that is, of the Lord." It could also refer to a hymn to Kyriak
or "Sunday." To these questions, the theories on the controversies withi
the ancient church have not yet found a definitive answer.

Like the image in the south hall that is in much better condition, th
struggle between the cock and the turtle has a symbolic meaning

Perhaps it simply refers to the struggle between good and evil. Lastly, the modest and schematic mosaic, followed by a graceful white rabbit, may have been the spot where the cathedra and the presbytery were located.

Now continue your tour along the centuries-old foundation. Do not forget to take a look at the most recent archaeological discoveries: the deep fountain and the beautiful mosaic that displays a six-pointed star. Before you leave the crypt by the same door through which you entered, you should devote your attention to the Cocciopesto floor and above all, the remainders of the mid-4th century, six-cornered post-theodorian baptistery on your left. As you ascend the modern stair-case, remain briefly at the small outer room between the basilica and the baptistry.

The Baptistry ⑫

Before you enter the baptistry of the Basilica, you will traverse a lon building which is connected to it. This is the so-called "Heathen Church" which received those waiting to be baptized. The building which was erected in the time of the Franks (9th century), was partiall torn down during the 18th century. Originally, it consisted of two sto ries, whose mostly lost upper story evidently resembled the lowe story that was dedicated to Saint Peter. A rectangular room with tw cross-vaults is connected to a square room with a domed vault. Th walls were adorned with fresco remnants from the 13th and 14th cen turies. The first room contains two niches, the second room, eight.

The baptistry, which was the third of its kind in Aquileia, is the resu of various changes and rearrangements. When it was built under B shop Chromatius (4th century), it featured a square floor plan. Late this floor plan was replaced by an octagonal one in order to recall th eighth day: the resurrection. Under Patriarch Maxentius (9th century the east-west axis, with its pivotal message, was installed. While th west refers to the darkness and the location of the sunset, the east the place of light and of the sunrise. The catachumens approach th baptismal font from the west, then exit the water and ultimately mov towards the location of the Eucharist in the east, the symbol of healin and of new life that had commenced with baptism. In the middle c the baptistry is a six-sided baptismal font, the result of a 19th-centur restoration. It is surrounded by six columns, which once supported shallow cover as well the ambulatory up to the side walls.

It is best to exit the baptistry via the small side door that leads yo directly to a large square. From there, you can reach the campanile whose peak offers an unforgettable view. Not only can you fathom th structural secrets of the Basilica and see the area where the remainin mosaics (now in storage in the Museo Acheologico Nazionale) of th North Church were discovered in the mid-20th century; in good wea ther, you can also see the amazing Friuli plains which are traverse by the Isonzo, Tagliamento, and Livenza rivers; from the Gulf c Trieste (?) over the raw karstic hills, the eastern and the western Ju lian Alps to the Carnic Alps and the Dolomites.

The Campanile (Bell tower) ⑬

The imposing campanile of Aquileia, which rises alongside the patriarchal basilica, was built in the first half of the 11th century under
Patriarch Poppo. As previously mentioned, the 4th century floor mosaics below it, now on display in the Excavation Crypt, were damaged
in the process.

According to an inscription which has unfortunately been lost, the
construction of a *turris celsa quod astra petit*, or "tower which is so
high that it reaches the stars" was one of the bishop's glorious accom-
plishments.

The campanile was a part of Poppo's project to reorganize and im-
prove the entire complex; alongside its liturgical function, it may
have served a defensive one as well. The tower was built with large
limestone blocks from Aurisina which may have come from a Roman
amphitheater.

In comparison to the other towers in North Italy, the campanile is
unusual in its combination of the classical tower of Western architecture with the unique pointed tower architecture of the east. Over the
course of centuries and as a result of countless fires and earthquakes,
the campanile was remodeled and rebuilt. In so doing, its original
appearance was partially altered. The total height of the campanile
currently adds up to 73 meters.

The Cemetery

After you have ascended the campani
you should take a look at the cemete
which is located behind the basilic
There, you will notice a quotation
Gabriele D'Annunzio, which is engrav
upon the church wall. It was dedicat
to Aquileia and the glorious heroes wl
perished during the First World War: '
Aquileia, donna di tristezza, sovrana
dolore, tu serbi le primizie della for
nei tumuli di zolle, all'ombra dei c
pressi pensierosi. Custodisci nell'erba
morti primi: una verginità di sangue s
cro e quasi un fiorire di martirio cl
rinnovella in te la melodia. La mad
chiama e in te comincia il canto. N
profondo di te comincia il canto. L'in
comincia degli imperituri quando il d
luvio calice s'innalza. Trema a tutti
viventi il cuore in petto. Il sacrific
arde fra l'Alpe e il mare."

These verses were originally carved in
a stone slab which was destroyed in tl
Battle of Kobarid in 1917. The ceme
tery which had been newly restructure
just a few months earlier was defile
with one hundred and fifty crosses wit
the inscription,*"Dulce Et Decorum E*
Pro Patria Mori." Of the thousands
World War I victims, many young so
diers were killed here; also buried her
were the mortal remains of ten un
known soldiers. The eleventh was bu
ied in the Basilica of Aquileia by
grieving mother, Maria Bergamas fro
Gradisca d'Isonzo, when she "recog
nized" her son. Since then, he has bee
laid to rest at the altar of his nativ

country at the National Memorial for Victor Emanuel II in Rome. Two imposing sculptures which emphasize the powerful impact of the cemetery are also worth noting: the *Pietà* by Edmondo Furlan and *Victim* by Ettore Ximenes.

The cemetery serves as a reminder of the absurdity of the wars of the 20th century, at a point in time when the "sacred borders" have been opened and Italy is proud to speak the European language of "United in Diversity."

Additional Points of Interest in Aquileia

If you still have time after your visit to the Basilica of Aquileia, then take a look at the city of Aquileia and its ruins from the Roman era.

Along the street which leads to Grado, upon the *"cardo maximus"* is the visible part of the Forum: the main square and center of the ecomonic, political, and social life of the Roman city of Aquileia.

A few steps further along, the remains of the inner harbor at the Via Sacra can be accessed. From the harbor, which was built along the original flow of the Natisone and Torre rivers, the west bridge, the warehouse foundations, the underpasses, and the city walls are still preserved.

It is also worth visiting the Museo Acheologico Nazionale and the Museo Paleocristiano in the Monastero district. The former contains one of the most significant archaeological collections within North Italy; the latter is located within a former Benedictine cloister that was built on top of an early Christian basilica on the city outskirts. In the Museo Paleocristiano, floor mosaics and wall fragments can be seen, whereas the wall mosaics originate from a later period. The 18th-century structural shell includes remnants from Aquileia of Late Antiquity and from the city of the patriarchs.

The various archaeological sites also merit attention: the Fondo ex Cossar with an "island" and currently-restored houses and possibly Early Christian oratorios decorated with fantastic mosaics, beneath that of the "good shepherd in unusual clothing"; the Fondo ex Cal with additional buildings, the thermae, the Sepolcreto with graves from the 1st to the 4th centuries A.D., and the Basilica of Beligna, whose mosaic fragments are also on display in the Museo Paleocristiano.

Translation: M. Dias-Hargarter

Chronology

181 B.C.	Romans establish military colony of Aquileia.
27 B.C. –14 A.D.	Aquileia becomes the capital of the 10th region (Venetia et Histria). Under the reign of Augustus, the city begins to experience a significant economic boost.
284–305 A.D.	Reign of Diocletian.
303–304 A.D.	Christians persecuted under Diocletian: martyrdom of the saints Cantianus, Protus, and Chrysogonus.
313 A.D.	The issue of the Edict of Milan, which brought Christians the freedom to choose their beliefs.
313–315 A.D.	Construction of the Basilica of Aquileia at the request of Bishop Theodore.
381 A.D.	Anti-Arian Council of Aquileia, in which the Bishop of Milan took part.
388–408 A.D.	Chromatius is the bishop of Aquileia.
452 A.D.	Aquileia is destroyed by the Huns, led by Attila The inhabitants flee to Grado, where the bishops eventually also seek shelter (Castrum Gradense).
553–699	Three-Chapter Controversy. Inter-church and political crisis, which led to the schism between the Churches of Aquileia and Rome, and induced the separation of the patriarchate: philo-Lombardy (located in Aquileia) and philo-Byzantine (located in Grado). In 568, Bishop Paul escapes to Grado with the treasures of the Church of Aquileia.
568	Invasion of the Lombards under the leadership of Alboin and establishment of the Lombard Empire.
787–802	Patriarchate of Paulinus. Lombard dominance ends and Carolingian rule begins.
811–817	Patriarchate of Maxentius: The Basilica is rebuilt according to the Roman style.
1019–1042	Patriarch Poppo oversees the construction of the medieval church to completion.
1077	The patriarch state gains legitimacy with the patriarchate of Sieghard.
1348	The basilica sustains severe damage from a major earthquake.
1368–1381	Patriarch Marquard von Randeck has the damaged church rebuilt in the Gothic style.
1420	Venetian takeover of Friuli and the end of the chronological reign of Aquileia's patriarchs.
1509	Aquileia is occupied by the Austrians.
1751	Permanent abolishment of the Aquileia patriarchate and subsequent formation of the archdioceses of Gorizia (1752) and Udine (1753).

Opening Hours

Opening Hours: Basilica of Aquileia

Summer: from the end of March until the end of October.
9:00 a.m. – 7:00 p.m. daily.
Winter 9:00 a.m. – 4:30 p.m., Sat., Sun.,
and public holidays 9:00 a.m.– 5:00 p.m.
Gift Shop: same opening hours as the Basilica.
Campanile: Summer: 9:30 a.m. – 1.30 p.m. and 3:30 p.m. – 6:30 p.m.
Winter: Closed.

Sunday Mass: 10:30 a.m.

Please note that opening hours are subject to change. Information
is available by dialing 0039 (0)431/91067 (Basilica) or 0039
(0)431/919719 (Office), via fax 0039 (0)431/919828 or via e-mail at
basilica.aquileia@virgilio.it

Museo Archeologico Nazionale

Year-round: Mon. 8:30 a.m. – 2:00 p.m. (Ticket office until 1:30),
Tues. to Sun. 8:30 a.m. – 7:30 p.m. (Ticket office open until 7:00 p.m.).

Archaeological Grounds

8:30 a.m. until one hour before sunset.

Museo Paleocristiano

Closed Mon.; Tue.– Sun. 8:30 a.m. – 1:45 p.m.
For information, call: 0039 (0)431/91016 and 0039 (0)431/91035 or
write to: info@museoarcheo-aquileia.it

Tourist information: 0039 (0)431/919491 and
info.aquileia@turismo.fvg.it
Pro Loco Aquileia (non-profit organization):
0039 (0)431/91087 and prolocoaquileia@libero.it

Foundation "Società per la Conservazione della Basilica di Aquileia"

The guide was compiled by Anna Maria Viganò and Sara Zamparo and
distributed as the official tourist guide of the Friuli-Venezia Giulia
region.
Thanks to Andrea Bellavite, Barbara Tomat and everyone who contribu-
ted to its completion.

Bibliography

- BRUSIN, G., **Aquileia e Grado, guida breve,** Padua, 1980.
- CADEDDU, L., **La Leggenda del Soldato Sconosciuto all'Altare della Patria,** Monfalco ne, 2001, pp. 175–180.
- DELLASORTE BRUMAT, **G., Aquileia e San Canzian,** Venice, 2005, pp. 3, 78 and 61–6
- FIACCADORI, G. (Hg.), **Arte in Friuli Venezia Giulia,** Udine, 1999, pp. 104–111.
- LEHMANN, T., Die ältesten erhaltenen Bilder in einem Kirchenbau. **Zu den frühchrist** chen Kirchenbauten und Mosaiken unter dem Dom von Aquileia, in: Das Altertum 2009, pp. 91–122.
- MARINI, G., **La Basilica Patriarcale di Aquileia,** 1994, pp. 56–58 and 102–104.
- MAROCCO, E., **Aquileia romana e cristiana,**Trieste, 2000, pp. 4–30.
- MICALI, B. – TOPPANI, B., **La Cappella Torriani (o di S. Ambrogio),** Sopraintendenza beni A.A.A.A .e S. del F.V.G.
- QUERCIOLI, M., **Aquileia, Il Bel Paese,** ITINERARI, Nr. 19, Rom, 2004, pp. 22–60.
- TAVANO, S., **Aquileia e Grado, storia-arte-cultura,** Trieste, 1986.
- TAVANO, S., **Aquileia, i Patriarchi e l'Europa,** Pasian di Prato, 2000.
- VIDULLI TORLO, M., **Aquileia mosaici,** Trieste, 2005, pp. 3, 11, 21, 25, 53, and 60.
- VON LANCKOROSKY, K., **La Basilica di Aquileia,** S. Tavano (Pub.), Vienna 1906, - Gö 2007, pp. 23–39, 112–135, and 159.
- ZOVATTO, P.L., Il **Santo Sepolcro di Aquileia e il Dramma Liturgico Medioevale,** Udir 1956.

Front Cover: The Basilica of Aquileia
Inside Cover: Floor Mosaic from the South Hall
Back Cover: Detail from the Jonah Mosaic

Photographs: Enzo Andrian – Fiumicello (UD)

Floor Plan: Cidin arch. Simona – Studio tecnico di progettazione arch. Carlo Cossar Aquileia (UD)

Subscription: Our "Kleine Kunstführer", guides to churches, castles and collections Europe, may be ordered on subscription from the publishers. The series was founded Dr. Hugo Schnell † and Dr. Johannes Steiner †.

Schnell, Art Guide Nr. 2744   1. Edition 20

© **VERLAG SCHNELL & STEINER GMBH REGENSBURG**

Leibnizstraße 13, D-93055 Regensburg
Telephone: +49 (0)941 7 87 85-0 · Telefax: +49 (0)941 7 87 85 16
Entire Production: Schnell & Steiner GmbH Regensburg
This work may not be reproduced in whole or in part

ISBN 978-3-7954-6837-8

Further information about our publications can be found under:
www.schnell-und-steiner.de